# Forget-Me-Not

An Avid Reader's
Book Tracking Journal

## Books I've Read

Susan A. Jennings

Forget-Me-Not
Book Tracking Journal


Cover image and Author photo: SAJ Design
Author photo interior the late Doris Leightley
Images: Shuttestock/ju_see and Shutterstock/Ulada

For more books, novels and journals
www.susanajennings.com

# MY

# Forget-Me-Not

# Book Tracking Journal

Name: ________________________________

Contact: ______________________________

Notes: ________________________________

_______________________________________

_______________________________________

_______________________________________

## Dedication

To all
the wonderful storytellers
and avid readers around the globe.

# Introduction

Dear Reader,

If you walked into my home today you would be surrounded by books. My study is lined with floor to ceiling bookcases plus a few piles of books waiting to be shelved. A stack or two of books sit on my dressingtable, mostly read with another stack to read next. The living room coffee table has more than it's fair share of novels and a few interesting biographies.

Collecting books is my passion, physical hard copy books. I flip the pages, smell the ink and feel the covers. Each book takes me on a journey, an intriging mystery or exciting adventure into the lives of characters who I love, hate or admire. Stories trigger my imagination, one could say, back into the fantasy that was so easy as a child. If you are reading this I am pretty sure you are nodding your head in agreement.

I do have an e-reader and embrace the new technology but there is nothing like holding a paper book firmly in my hand.

I consider it to be sacrelidge to throw a book away, so those I have no room for or perhaps were not my favourites I give away or donate.

But, it became a challenge to remember all the books and series' I've read and sometimes expensive and disappointing as I bought titles I had already read, publishers and authors often change the covers.

I had an idea and designed a reader's book tracking journal

The result was this small, easy to use book tracking journal, which I am delighted to share with you.

Happy reading,

Susan

"Books to the ceiling, books to the sky,
My pile of books is a mile high.
How I love them! How I need them!
I'll have a long beard by the time
I read them."

- Arnold Lobel

# Forget-Me-Not Book Tracking

## Easy to use Suggestions

- Add the title, author, genre, format and number of pages
- Name the series, note the number of books in the series
- Note the date you started and the date you finished a book
- Rate the book by filling in the mini books.
- 1 being poor and 5 being excellent
- Note your opinion of the story
- Write a review and add your thoughts
- Jot down the book's theme and how it made you feel
- When and where did you buy this book?
- Where were you when you read the book?
- List your own table of contents as you review your books
- Note if you would recommend this book
- And, to whom

# Table of Content

| Page # | Book Title & Author |
|---|---|

# Table of Content

| Page # | Book Title & Author |
|---|---|

# My Review and Thoughts

# Book Details

**Title:** ____________________

Subtitle: ____________________

Author: ____________________

Genre: ______________ #Pages______

Series: ____________________

How many in series? ______________

Next book in series ______________

Format: Print E-Book Audio PDF

Bought/Borrowed from ______________

Date started ____________ Finished ________

How would you rate this book?

Fill in the mini books - 1= Poor and 5 = Excellent

This book made me feel...

Happy Sad Angry Grateful Loving Disturbed

In your opnion rate the following...

Quality of writing ______________

Engaging plot ______________

Suspenseful ______________

Believable characters ______________

Would you recommend this book? Yes No Maybe

# My Review and Thoughts

## Book Details

**Title:** ______________________________

Subtitle: ______________________________

Author: ______________________________

Genre: ____________________ #Pages__________

Series: ______________________________

How many in series? ____________________

Next book in series ____________________

Format: Print E-Book Audio PDF

Bought/Borrowed from ____________________

Date started ______________ Finished __________

How would you rate this book?

Fill in the mini books - 1= Poor and 5 = Excellent

This book made me feel...

Happy Sad Angry Grateful Loving Disturbed

In your opnion rate the following...

Quality of writing ____________________

Engaging plot ____________________

Suspenseful ____________________

Believable characters ____________________

Would you recommend this book? Yes No Maybe

# My Review and Thoughts

# Book Details

**Title:** ____________________

Subtitle: ____________________

Author: ____________________

Genre: ____________________ #Pages__________

Series: ____________________

How many in series? ____________________

Next book in series ____________________

Format: Print E-Book Audio PDF

Bought/Borrowed from ____________________

Date started ______________ Finished ______________

How would you rate this book?

Fill in the mini books - 1= Poor and 5 = Excellent

This book made me feel...

Happy Sad Angry Grateful Loving Disturbed

In your opnion rate the following...

Quality of writing ____________________

Engaging plot ____________________

Suspenseful ____________________

Believable characters ____________________

Would you recommend this book? Yes No Maybe

# My Review and Thoughts

# Book Details

**Title:** ____________________

Subtitle: ____________________

Author: ____________________

Genre: ______________ #Pages________

Series: ____________________

How many in series? ______________

Next book in series ______________

Format: Print E-Book Audio PDF

Bought/Borrowed from ______________

Date started __________ Finished __________

How would you rate this book?

Fill in the mini books - 1= Poor and 5 = Excellent

This book made me feel...

Happy Sad Angry Grateful Loving Disturbed

In your opnion rate the following...

Quality of writing ______________

Engaging plot ______________

Suspenseful ______________

Believable characters ______________

Would you recommend this book? Yes No Maybe

# My Review and Thoughts

## Book Details

Title: ______________________________

Subtitle: ______________________________

Author: ______________________________

Genre: ____________________ #Pages__________

Series: ______________________________

How many in series? ______________________

Next book in series ______________________

Format: Print E-Book Audio PDF

Bought/Borrowed from ____________________

Date started ______________ Finished __________

How would you rate this book?

Fill in the mini books - 1= Poor and 5 = Excellent

This book made me feel...

Happy Sad Angry Grateful Loving Disturbed

In your opnion rate the following...

Quality of writing ______________________

Engaging plot ______________________

Suspenseful ______________________

Believable characters ______________________

Would you recommend this book? Yes No Maybe

# My Review and Thoughts

# Book Details

**Title:** ______________________________

Subtitle: ______________________________

Author: ______________________________

Genre: ____________________ #Pages__________

Series: ______________________________

How many in series? ____________________

Next book in series ____________________

Format: Print E-Book Audio PDF

Bought/Borrowed from ____________________

Date started ______________ Finished __________

How would you rate this book?

Fill in the mini books - 1= Poor and 5 = Excellent

This book made me feel...

Happy Sad Angry Grateful Loving Disturbed

In your opnion rate the following...

Quality of writing ____________________

Engaging plot ____________________

Suspenseful ____________________

Believable characters ____________________

Would you recommend this book? Yes No Maybe

# My Review and Thoughts

# Book Details

Title: ______________________________

Subtitle: ______________________________

Author: ______________________________

Genre: ____________________ #Pages__________

Series: ______________________________

How many in series? ______________________

Next book in series ______________________

Format: Print E-Book Audio PDF

Bought/Borrowed from ____________________

Date started ______________ Finished __________

How would you rate this book?

Fill in the mini books - 1= Poor and 5 = Excellent

This book made me feel...

Happy Sad Angry Grateful Loving Disturbed

In your opnion rate the following...

Quality of writing ______________________

Engaging plot ______________________

Suspenseful ______________________

Believable characters ______________________

Would you recommend this book? Yes No Maybe

# My Review and Thoughts

# Book Details

**Title:** ______________________________

Subtitle: ______________________________

Author: ______________________________

Genre: ____________________ #Pages__________

Series: ______________________________

How many in series? ____________________

Next book in series ____________________

Format: Print E-Book Audio PDF

Bought/Borrowed from ____________________

Date started ______________ Finished __________

How would you rate this book?

Fill in the mini books - 1= Poor and 5 = Excellent

This book made me feel...

Happy Sad Angry Grateful Loving Disturbed

In your opnion rate the following...

Quality of writing ____________________

Engaging plot ____________________

Suspenseful ____________________

Believable characters ____________________

Would you recommend this book? Yes No Maybe

# My Review and Thoughts

# Book Details

**Title:** ______________________________

Subtitle: ______________________________

Author: ______________________________

Genre: ____________________ #Pages__________

Series: ______________________________

How many in series? ____________________

Next book in series ____________________

Format: Print E-Book Audio PDF

Bought/Borrowed from ____________________

Date started ______________ Finished __________

How would you rate this book?

Fill in the mini books - 1= Poor and 5 = Excellent

This book made me feel...

Happy Sad Angry Grateful Loving Disturbed

In your opnion rate the following...

Quality of writing ____________________

Engaging plot ____________________

Suspenseful ____________________

Believable characters ____________________

Would you recommend this book? Yes No Maybe

# My Review and Thoughts

# Book Details

Title: ______________________________

Subtitle: ______________________________

Author: ______________________________

Genre: ____________________ #Pages__________

Series: ______________________________

How many in series? ______________________

Next book in series ______________________

Format: Print E-Book Audio PDF

Bought/Borrowed from ____________________

Date started ______________ Finished __________

How would you rate this book?

Fill in the mini books - 1= Poor and 5 = Excellent

This book made me feel...

Happy Sad Angry Grateful Loving Disturbed

In your opnion rate the following...

Quality of writing ______________________

Engaging plot ______________________

Suspenseful ______________________

Believable characters ______________________

Would you recommend this book? Yes No Maybe

# My Review and Thoughts

# Book Details

**Title:** ______________________________

Subtitle: ______________________________

Author: ______________________________

Genre: ____________________ #Pages__________

Series: ______________________________

How many in series? ____________________

Next book in series ____________________

Format: Print E-Book Audio PDF

Bought/Borrowed from ____________________

Date started ______________ Finished ____________

How would you rate this book?

Fill in the mini books - 1= Poor and 5 = Excellent

This book made me feel...

Happy Sad Angry Grateful Loving Disturbed

In your opnion rate the following...

Quality of writing ____________________

Engaging plot ____________________

Suspenseful ____________________

Believable characters ____________________

Would you recommend this book? Yes No Maybe

# My Review and Thoughts

# Book Details

**Title:** ______________________________

Subtitle: ______________________________

Author: ______________________________

Genre: ____________________ #Pages__________

Series: ______________________________

How many in series? ____________________

Next book in series ____________________

Format: Print E-Book Audio PDF

Bought/Borrowed from ____________________

Date started ______________ Finished __________

How would you rate this book?

Fill in the mini books - 1= Poor and 5 = Excellent

This book made me feel...

Happy Sad Angry Grateful Loving Disturbed

In your opnion rate the following...

Quality of writing ____________________

Engaging plot ____________________

Suspenseful ____________________

Believable characters ____________________

Would you recommend this book? Yes No Maybe

# My Review and Thoughts

# Book Details

**Title:** ______________________________

Subtitle: ______________________________

Author: ______________________________

Genre: ____________________ #Pages__________

Series: ______________________________

How many in series? ____________________

Next book in series ____________________

Format: Print E-Book Audio PDF

Bought/Borrowed from ____________________

Date started ______________ Finished ___________

How would you rate this book?

Fill in the mini books - 1= Poor and 5 = Excellent

This book made me feel...

Happy Sad Angry Grateful Loving Disturbed

In your opnion rate the following...

Quality of writing ____________________

Engaging plot ____________________

Suspenseful ____________________

Believable characters ____________________

Would you recommend this book? Yes No Maybe

# My Review and Thoughts

# Book Details

**Title:** ________________________________

Subtitle: ________________________________

Author: ________________________________

Genre: ____________________ #Pages__________

Series: ________________________________

How many in series? ______________________

Next book in series ______________________

Format: Print E-Book Audio PDF

Bought/Borrowed from ____________________

Date started ______________ Finished __________

How would you rate this book?

Fill in the mini books - 1= Poor and 5 = Excellent

This book made me feel...

Happy Sad Angry Grateful Loving Disturbed

In your opnion rate the following...

Quality of writing ______________________

Engaging plot ______________________

Suspenseful ______________________

Believable characters ______________________

Would you recommend this book? Yes No Maybe

# My Review and Thoughts

# Book Details

Title: ____________________________

Subtitle: ____________________________

Author: ____________________________

Genre: ________________ #Pages________

Series: ____________________________

How many in series? ____________________

Next book in series ____________________

Format: Print E-Book Audio PDF

Bought/Borrowed from ____________________

Date started ____________ Finished __________

How would you rate this book?

Fill in the mini books - 1= Poor and 5 = Excellent

This book made me feel...

Happy Sad Angry Grateful Loving Disturbed

In your opnion rate the following...

Quality of writing ____________________

Engaging plot ____________________

Suspenseful ____________________

Believable characters ____________________

Would you recommend this book? Yes No Maybe

# My Review and Thoughts

# Book Details

Title: ______________________________

Subtitle: ______________________________

Author: ______________________________

Genre: ____________________ #Pages__________

Series: ______________________________

How many in series? ____________________

Next book in series ____________________

Format: Print E-Book Audio PDF

Bought/Borrowed from ____________________

Date started ______________ Finished __________

How would you rate this book?

Fill in the mini books - 1= Poor and 5 = Excellent

This book made me feel...

Happy Sad Angry Grateful Loving Disturbed

In your opnion rate the following...

Quality of writing ____________________

Engaging plot ____________________

Suspenseful ____________________

Believable characters ____________________

Would you recommend this book? Yes No Maybe

# My Review and Thoughts

## Book Details

**Title:** ______________________

Subtitle: ______________________

Author: ______________________

Genre: ______________ #Pages__________

Series: ______________________

How many in series? ______________________

Next book in series ______________________

Format: Print E-Book Audio PDF

Bought/Borrowed from ______________________

Date started ______________ Finished __________

How would you rate this book?

Fill in the mini books - 1= Poor and 5 = Excellent

This book made me feel...

Happy Sad Angry Grateful Loving Disturbed

In your opnion rate the following...

Quality of writing ______________________

Engaging plot ______________________

Suspenseful ______________________

Believable characters ______________________

Would you recommend this book? Yes No Maybe

# My Review and Thoughts

# Book Details

**Title:** ______________________________

Subtitle: ______________________________

Author: ______________________________

Genre: ____________________ #Pages__________

Series: ______________________________

How many in series? ____________________

Next book in series ____________________

Format: Print E-Book Audio PDF

Bought/Borrowed from ____________________

Date started ______________ Finished __________

How would you rate this book?

Fill in the mini books - 1= Poor and 5 = Excellent

This book made me feel...

Happy Sad Angry Grateful Loving Disturbed

In your opnion rate the following...

Quality of writing ____________________

Engaging plot ____________________

Suspenseful ____________________

Believable characters ____________________

Would you recommend this book? Yes No Maybe

# My Review and Thoughts

# Book Details

**Title:** ______________________________

Subtitle: ______________________________

Author: ______________________________

Genre: ____________________ #Pages__________

Series: ______________________________

How many in series? ____________________

Next book in series ____________________

Format: Print E-Book Audio PDF

Bought/Borrowed from ____________________

Date started ______________ Finished __________

How would you rate this book?

Fill in the mini books - 1= Poor and 5 = Excellent

This book made me feel...

Happy Sad Angry Grateful Loving Disturbed

In your opnion rate the following...

Quality of writing ____________________

Engaging plot ____________________

Suspenseful ____________________

Believable characters ____________________

Would you recommend this book? Yes No Maybe

# My Review and Thoughts

# Book Details

**Title:** ______________________________

Subtitle: ______________________________

Author: ______________________________

Genre: ____________________ #Pages__________

Series: ______________________________

How many in series? ______________________

Next book in series ______________________

Format: Print E-Book Audio PDF

Bought/Borrowed from ____________________

Date started ______________ Finished __________

How would you rate this book?

Fill in the mini books - 1= Poor and 5 = Excellent

This book made me feel...

Happy Sad Angry Grateful Loving Disturbed

In your opnion rate the following...

Quality of writing ______________________

Engaging plot ______________________

Suspenseful ______________________

Believable characters ______________________

Would you recommend this book? Yes No Maybe

# My Review and Thoughts

# Book Details

Title: ______________________

Subtitle: ______________________

Author: ______________________

Genre: ______________ #Pages________

Series: ______________________

How many in series? ______________

Next book in series ______________

Format: Print E-Book Audio PDF

Bought/Borrowed from ______________

Date started __________ Finished __________

How would you rate this book?

Fill in the mini books - 1= Poor and 5 = Excellent

This book made me feel...

Happy Sad Angry Grateful Loving Disturbed

In your opnion rate the following...

Quality of writing ______________

Engaging plot ______________

Suspenseful ______________

Believable characters ______________

Would you recommend this book? Yes No Maybe

# My Review and Thoughts

# Book Details

**Title:** ______________________

Subtitle: ______________________

Author: ______________________

Genre: ______________ #Pages ________

Series: ______________________

How many in series? ______________

Next book in series ______________

Format: Print E-Book Audio PDF

Bought/Borrowed from ______________

Date started ____________ Finished ________

How would you rate this book?

Fill in the mini books - 1= Poor and 5 = Excellent

This book made me feel...

Happy Sad Angry Grateful Loving Disturbed

In your opnion rate the following...

Quality of writing ______________

Engaging plot ______________

Suspenseful ______________

Believable characters ______________

Would you recommend this book? Yes No Maybe

# My Review and Thoughts

# Book Details

Title: ______________________________

Subtitle: ______________________________

Author: ______________________________

Genre: ____________________ #Pages__________

Series: ______________________________

How many in series? ______________________

Next book in series ______________________

Format: Print E-Book Audio PDF

Bought/Borrowed from ____________________

Date started ______________ Finished ___________

How would you rate this book?

Fill in the mini books - 1= Poor and 5 = Excellent

This book made me feel...

Happy Sad Angry Grateful Loving Disturbed

In your opnion rate the following...

Quality of writing ______________________

Engaging plot ______________________

Suspenseful ______________________

Believable characters ______________________

Would you recommend this book? Yes No Maybe

# My Review and Thoughts

## Book Details

**Title:** ____________________

Subtitle: ____________________

Author: ____________________

Genre: ____________________ #Pages__________

Series: ____________________

How many in series? ____________________

Next book in series ____________________

Format: Print E-Book Audio PDF

Bought/Borrowed from ____________________

Date started ______________ Finished __________

How would you rate this book?

Fill in the mini books - 1= Poor and 5 = Excellent

This book made me feel...

Happy Sad Angry Grateful Loving Disturbed

In your opnion rate the following...

Quality of writing ____________________

Engaging plot ____________________

Suspenseful ____________________

Believable characters ____________________

Would you recommend this book? Yes No Maybe

# My Review and Thoughts

# Book Details

Title: ______________________________

Subtitle: ______________________________

Author: ______________________________

Genre: ____________________ #Pages__________

Series: ______________________________

How many in series? ____________________

Next book in series ____________________

Format: Print E-Book Audio PDF

Bought/Borrowed from ____________________

Date started ______________ Finished __________

How would you rate this book?

Fill in the mini books - 1= Poor and 5 = Excellent

This book made me feel...

Happy Sad Angry Grateful Loving Disturbed

In your opnion rate the following...

Quality of writing ____________________

Engaging plot ____________________

Suspenseful ____________________

Believable characters ____________________

Would you recommend this book? Yes No Maybe

# My Review and Thoughts

# Book Details

Title: ______________________________

Subtitle: ______________________________

Author: ______________________________

Genre: ____________________ #Pages__________

Series: ______________________________

How many in series? ______________________

Next book in series ______________________

Format: Print E-Book Audio PDF

Bought/Borrowed from ____________________

Date started ______________ Finished __________

How would you rate this book?

Fill in the mini books - 1= Poor and 5 = Excellent

This book made me feel...

Happy Sad Angry Grateful Loving Disturbed

In your opnion rate the following...

Quality of writing ______________________

Engaging plot ______________________

Suspenseful ______________________

Believable characters ______________________

Would you recommend this book? Yes No Maybe

# My Review and Thoughts

# Book Details

**Title:** ______________________________

Subtitle: ______________________________

Author: ______________________________

Genre: ____________________ #Pages__________

Series: ______________________________

How many in series? ____________________

Next book in series ____________________

Format: Print E-Book Audio PDF

Bought/Borrowed from ____________________

Date started ______________ Finished __________

How would you rate this book?

Fill in the mini books - 1= Poor and 5 = Excellent

This book made me feel...

Happy Sad Angry Grateful Loving Disturbed

In your opnion rate the following...

Quality of writing ____________________

Engaging plot ____________________

Suspenseful ____________________

Believable characters ____________________

Would you recommend this book? Yes No Maybe

# My Review and Thoughts

# Book Details

Title: ____________________

Subtitle: ____________________

Author: ____________________

Genre: ____________ #Pages________

Series: ____________________

How many in series? ____________

Next book in series ____________

Format: Print E-Book Audio PDF

Bought/Borrowed from ____________

Date started ____________ Finished ________

How would you rate this book?

Fill in the mini books - 1= Poor and 5 = Excellent

This book made me feel...

Happy Sad Angry Grateful Loving Disturbed

In your opnion rate the following...

Quality of writing ____________

Engaging plot ____________

Suspenseful ____________

Believable characters ____________

Would you recommend this book? Yes No Maybe

# My Review and Thoughts

# Book Details

**Title:** ______________________________

Subtitle: ______________________________

Author: ______________________________

Genre: ____________________ #Pages__________

Series: ______________________________

How many in series? ______________________

Next book in series ______________________

Format: Print E-Book Audio PDF

Bought/Borrowed from ____________________

Date started ______________ Finished __________

How would you rate this book?

Fill in the mini books - 1= Poor and 5 = Excellent

This book made me feel...

Happy Sad Angry Grateful Loving Disturbed

In your opnion rate the following...

Quality of writing ______________________

Engaging plot ______________________

Suspenseful ______________________

Believable characters ______________________

Would you recommend this book? Yes No Maybe

# My Review and Thoughts

# Book Details

Title: ____________________

Subtitle: ____________________

Author: ____________________

Genre: ____________________ #Pages__________

Series: ____________________

How many in series? ____________________

Next book in series ____________________

Format: Print E-Book Audio PDF

Bought/Borrowed from ____________________

Date started ______________ Finished __________

How would you rate this book?

Fill in the mini books - 1= Poor and 5 = Excellent

This book made me feel...

Happy Sad Angry Grateful Loving Disturbed

In your opnion rate the following...

Quality of writing ____________________

Engaging plot ____________________

Suspenseful ____________________

Believable characters ____________________

Would you recommend this book? Yes No Maybe

# My Review and Thoughts

# Book Details

Title: ________________________________

Subtitle: ________________________________

Author: ________________________________

Genre: ____________________ #Pages__________

Series: ________________________________

How many in series? ________________________

Next book in series ________________________

Format: Print E-Book Audio PDF

Bought/Borrowed from ____________________

Date started ______________ Finished __________

How would you rate this book?

Fill in the mini books - 1= Poor and 5 = Excellent

This book made me feel...

Happy Sad Angry Grateful Loving Disturbed

In your opnion rate the following...

Quality of writing ________________________

Engaging plot ________________________

Suspenseful ________________________

Believable characters ________________________

Would you recommend this book? Yes No Maybe

# My Review and Thoughts

# Book Details

**Title:** ______________________________

Subtitle: ______________________________

Author: ______________________________

Genre: ____________________ #Pages__________

Series: ______________________________

How many in series? ____________________

Next book in series ____________________

Format: Print E-Book Audio PDF

Bought/Borrowed from ____________________

Date started ______________ Finished ___________

How would you rate this book?

Fill in the mini books - 1= Poor and 5 = Excellent

This book made me feel...

Happy Sad Angry Grateful Loving Disturbed

In your opnion rate the following...

Quality of writing ______________________________

Engaging plot ______________________________

Suspenseful ______________________________

Believable characters ____________________

Would you recommend this book? Yes No Maybe

# My Review and Thoughts

# Book Details

**Title:** ______________________________

Subtitle: ______________________________

Author: ______________________________

Genre: ____________________ #Pages__________

Series: ______________________________

How many in series? ______________________

Next book in series ______________________

Format: Print E-Book Audio PDF

Bought/Borrowed from ____________________

Date started ______________ Finished __________

How would you rate this book?

Fill in the mini books - 1= Poor and 5 = Excellent

This book made me feel...

Happy Sad Angry Grateful Loving Disturbed

In your opnion rate the following...

Quality of writing ______________________

Engaging plot ______________________

Suspenseful ______________________

Believable characters ______________________

Would you recommend this book? Yes No Maybe

# My Review and Thoughts

# Book Details

Title: ______________________________

Subtitle: ______________________________

Author: ______________________________

Genre: ____________________ #Pages__________

Series: ______________________________

How many in series? ______________________

Next book in series ______________________

Format: Print E-Book Audio PDF

Bought/Borrowed from ____________________

Date started ______________ Finished __________

How would you rate this book?

Fill in the mini books - 1= Poor and 5 = Excellent

This book made me feel...

Happy Sad Angry Grateful Loving Disturbed

In your opnion rate the following...

Quality of writing ________________________

Engaging plot ____________________________

Suspenseful ______________________________

Believable characters ______________________

Would you recommend this book? Yes No Maybe

# My Review and Thoughts

# Book Details

**Title:** ______________________________

Subtitle: ______________________________

Author: ______________________________

Genre: ____________________ #Pages__________

Series: ______________________________

How many in series? ______________________

Next book in series ______________________

Format: Print E-Book Audio PDF

Bought/Borrowed from ____________________

Date started ______________ Finished __________

How would you rate this book?

Fill in the mini books - 1= Poor and 5 = Excellent

This book made me feel...

Happy Sad Angry Grateful Loving Disturbed

In your opnion rate the following...

Quality of writing ______________________

Engaging plot ______________________

Suspenseful ______________________

Believable characters ______________________

Would you recommend this book? Yes No Maybe

# My Review and Thoughts

# Book Details

**Title:** ______________________________

Subtitle: ______________________________

Author: ______________________________

Genre: ____________________ #Pages__________

Series: ______________________________

How many in series? ______________________

Next book in series ______________________

Format: Print E-Book Audio PDF

Bought/Borrowed from ____________________

Date started ______________ Finished __________

How would you rate this book?

Fill in the mini books - 1= Poor and 5 = Excellent

This book made me feel...

Happy Sad Angry Grateful Loving Disturbed

In your opnion rate the following...

Quality of writing ______________________

Engaging plot ______________________

Suspenseful ______________________

Believable characters ______________________

Would you recommend this book? Yes No Maybe

# My Review and Thoughts

# Book Details

**Title:** ____________________

Subtitle: ____________________

Author: ____________________

Genre: ____________________ #Pages__________

Series: ____________________

How many in series? ____________________

Next book in series ____________________

Format: Print E-Book Audio PDF

Bought/Borrowed from ____________________

Date started ______________ Finished __________

How would you rate this book?

Fill in the mini books - 1= Poor and 5 = Excellent

This book made me feel...

Happy Sad Angry Grateful Loving Disturbed

In your opnion rate the following...

Quality of writing ____________________

Engaging plot ____________________

Suspenseful ____________________

Believable characters ____________________

Would you recommend this book? Yes No Maybe

# My Review and Thoughts

# Book Details

Title: ______________________

Subtitle: ______________________

Author: ______________________

Genre: ______________ #Pages__________

Series: ______________________

How many in series? ______________

Next book in series ______________

Format: Print E-Book Audio PDF

Bought/Borrowed from ______________

Date started ____________ Finished __________

How would you rate this book?

Fill in the mini books - 1= Poor and 5 = Excellent

This book made me feel...

Happy Sad Angry Grateful Loving Disturbed

In your opnion rate the following...

Quality of writing ______________

Engaging plot ______________

Suspenseful ______________

Believable characters ______________

Would you recommend this book? Yes No Maybe

# My Review and Thoughts

# Book Details

Title: ______________________

Subtitle: ______________________

Author: ______________________

Genre: ______________ #Pages________

Series: ______________________

How many in series? ______________

Next book in series ______________

Format: Print E-Book Audio PDF

Bought/Borrowed from ______________

Date started __________ Finished ________

How would you rate this book?

Fill in the mini books - 1= Poor and 5 = Excellent

This book made me feel...

Happy Sad Angry Grateful Loving Disturbed

In your opnion rate the following...

Quality of writing ______________

Engaging plot ______________

Suspenseful ______________

Believable characters ______________

Would you recommend this book? Yes No Maybe

# My Review and Thoughts

# Book Details

**Title:** ______________________________

Subtitle: ______________________________

Author: ______________________________

Genre: ____________________ #Pages________

Series: ______________________________

How many in series? ____________________

Next book in series ____________________

Format: Print E-Book Audio PDF

Bought/Borrowed from ____________________

Date started ______________ Finished ___________

How would you rate this book?

Fill in the mini books - 1= Poor and 5 = Excellent

This book made me feel...

Happy Sad Angry Grateful Loving Disturbed

In your opnion rate the following...

Quality of writing ____________________

Engaging plot ____________________

Suspenseful ____________________

Believable characters ____________________

Would you recommend this book? Yes No Maybe

# My Review and Thoughts

# Book Details

**Title:** ______________________________

Subtitle: ______________________________

Author: ______________________________

Genre: ____________________ #Pages__________

Series: ______________________________

How many in series? ______________________

Next book in series ______________________

Format: Print E-Book Audio PDF

Bought/Borrowed from ____________________

Date started ______________ Finished __________

How would you rate this book?

Fill in the mini books - 1= Poor and 5 = Excellent

This book made me feel...

Happy Sad Angry Grateful Loving Disturbed

In your opnion rate the following...

Quality of writing ______________________

Engaging plot ______________________

Suspenseful ______________________

Believable characters ______________________

Would you recommend this book? Yes No Maybe

# My Review and Thoughts

# Book Details

Title: ______________________________

Subtitle: ______________________________

Author: ______________________________

Genre: ____________________ #Pages__________

Series: ______________________________

How many in series? ______________________

Next book in series ______________________

Format: Print E-Book Audio PDF

Bought/Borrowed from ____________________

Date started ______________ Finished __________

How would you rate this book?

Fill in the mini books - 1= Poor and 5 = Excellent

This book made me feel...

Happy Sad Angry Grateful Loving Disturbed

In your opnion rate the following...

Quality of writing ______________________

Engaging plot ______________________

Suspenseful ______________________

Believable characters ______________________

Would you recommend this book? Yes No Maybe

# My Review and Thoughts

# Book Details

**Title:** ____________________

Subtitle: ____________________

Author: ____________________

Genre: ____________________ #Pages__________

Series: ____________________

How many in series? ____________________

Next book in series ____________________

Format: Print E-Book Audio PDF

Bought/Borrowed from ____________________

Date started ______________ Finished __________

How would you rate this book?

Fill in the mini books - 1= Poor and 5 = Excellent

This book made me feel...

Happy Sad Angry Grateful Loving Disturbed

In your opnion rate the following...

Quality of writing ____________________

Engaging plot ____________________

Suspenseful ____________________

Believable characters ____________________

Would you recommend this book? Yes No Maybe

# My Review and Thoughts

# Book Details

**Title:** ______________________________

Subtitle: ______________________________

Author: ______________________________

Genre: ____________________ #Pages__________

Series: ______________________________

How many in series? ______________________________

Next book in series ______________________________

Format: Print E-Book Audio PDF

Bought/Borrowed from ______________________________

Date started ______________ Finished ___________

How would you rate this book?

Fill in the mini books - 1= Poor and 5 = Excellent

This book made me feel...

Happy Sad Angry Grateful Loving Disturbed

In your opnion rate the following...

Quality of writing ______________________________

Engaging plot ______________________________

Suspenseful ______________________________

Believable characters ______________________________

Would you recommend this book? Yes No Maybe

# My Review and Thoughts

# Book Details

Title: ____________________

Subtitle: ____________________

Author: ____________________

Genre: ____________________ #Pages__________

Series: ____________________

How many in series? ____________________

Next book in series ____________________

Format: Print E-Book Audio PDF

Bought/Borrowed from ____________________

Date started ______________ Finished __________

How would you rate this book?

Fill in the mini books - 1= Poor and 5 = Excellent

This book made me feel...

Happy Sad Angry Grateful Loving Disturbed

In your opnion rate the following...

Quality of writing ____________________

Engaging plot ____________________

Suspenseful ____________________

Believable characters ____________________

Would you recommend this book? Yes No Maybe

# My Review and Thoughts

# Book Details

**Title:** ______________________________

Subtitle: ______________________________

Author: ______________________________

Genre: ____________________ #Pages __________

Series: ______________________________

How many in series? ______________________

Next book in series ______________________

Format: Print E-Book Audio PDF

Bought/Borrowed from ____________________

Date started ______________ Finished __________

How would you rate this book?

Fill in the mini books - 1= Poor and 5 = Excellent

This book made me feel...

Happy Sad Angry Grateful Loving Disturbed

In your opnion rate the following...

Quality of writing ______________________

Engaging plot ______________________

Suspenseful ______________________

Believable characters ______________________

Would you recommend this book? Yes No Maybe

# My Review and Thoughts

## Book Details

**Title:** ____________________

Subtitle: ____________________

Author: ____________________

Genre: ______________ #Pages ________

Series: ____________________

How many in series? ________________

Next book in series ________________

Format: Print E-Book Audio PDF

Bought/Borrowed from ________________

Date started ____________ Finished ___________

How would you rate this book?

Fill in the mini books - 1= Poor and 5 = Excellent

This book made me feel...

Happy Sad Angry Grateful Loving Disturbed

In your opnion rate the following...

Quality of writing ________________

Engaging plot ________________

Suspenseful ________________

Believable characters ________________

Would you recommend this book? Yes No Maybe

# My Review and Thoughts

# Book Details

**Title:** ______________________________

Subtitle: ______________________________

Author: ______________________________

Genre: ________________ #Pages________

Series: ______________________________

How many in series? ____________________

Next book in series ____________________

Format: Print E-Book Audio PDF

Bought/Borrowed from ____________________

Date started ____________ Finished __________

How would you rate this book?

Fill in the mini books - 1= Poor and 5 = Excellent

This book made me feel...

Happy Sad Angry Grateful Loving Disturbed

In your opnion rate the following...

Quality of writing ____________________

Engaging plot ____________________

Suspenseful ____________________

Believable characters ____________________

Would you recommend this book? Yes No Maybe

# My Review and Thoughts

# Book Details

Title: ______________________________

Subtitle: ______________________________

Author: ______________________________

Genre: ____________________ #Pages__________

Series: ______________________________

How many in series? ____________________

Next book in series ____________________

Format: Print E-Book Audio PDF

Bought/Borrowed from ____________________

Date started ______________ Finished __________

How would you rate this book?

Fill in the mini books - 1= Poor and 5 = Excellent

This book made me feel...

Happy Sad Angry Grateful Loving Disturbed

In your opnion rate the following...

Quality of writing ______________________________

Engaging plot ______________________________

Suspenseful ______________________________

Believable characters ______________________________

Would you recommend this book? Yes No Maybe

# My Review and Thoughts

# Book Details

**Title:** ______________________________

Subtitle: ______________________________

Author: ______________________________

Genre: ____________________ #Pages__________

Series: ______________________________

How many in series? ____________________

Next book in series ____________________

Format: Print E-Book Audio PDF

Bought/Borrowed from ____________________

Date started ______________ Finished __________

How would you rate this book?

Fill in the mini books - 1= Poor and 5 = Excellent

This book made me feel...

Happy Sad Angry Grateful Loving Disturbed

In your opnion rate the following...

Quality of writing ______________________________

Engaging plot ______________________________

Suspenseful ______________________________

Believable characters ____________________

Would you recommend this book? Yes No Maybe

# My Review and Thoughts

# Book Details

**Title:** ______________________________

Subtitle: ______________________________

Author: ______________________________

Genre: ____________________ #Pages__________

Series: ______________________________

How many in series? ______________________

Next book in series ______________________

Format: Print E-Book Audio PDF

Bought/Borrowed from ____________________

Date started _______________ Finished __________

How would you rate this book?

Fill in the mini books - 1= Poor and 5 = Excellent

This book made me feel...

Happy Sad Angry Grateful Loving Disturbed

In your opnion rate the following...

Quality of writing ______________________

Engaging plot ______________________

Suspenseful ______________________

Believable characters ______________________

Would you recommend this book? Yes No Maybe

# My Review and Thoughts

# Book Details

Title: ______________________

Subtitle: ______________________

Author: ______________________

Genre: ______________ #Pages________

Series: ______________________

How many in series? ______________

Next book in series ______________

Format: Print E-Book Audio PDF

Bought/Borrowed from ______________

Date started ____________ Finished __________

How would you rate this book?

Fill in the mini books - 1= Poor and 5 = Excellent

This book made me feel...

Happy Sad Angry Grateful Loving Disturbed

In your opnion rate the following...

Quality of writing ______________

Engaging plot ______________

Suspenseful ______________

Believable characters ______________

Would you recommend this book? Yes No Maybe

# My Review and Thoughts

# Book Details

Title: ______________________________

Subtitle: ______________________________

Author: ______________________________

Genre: ____________________ #Pages__________

Series: ______________________________

How many in series? ______________________________

Next book in series ______________________________

Format: Print E-Book Audio PDF

Bought/Borrowed from ______________________________

Date started ______________ Finished ___________

How would you rate this book?

Fill in the mini books - 1= Poor and 5 = Excellent

This book made me feel...

Happy Sad Angry Grateful Loving Disturbed

In your opnion rate the following...

Quality of writing ______________________________

Engaging plot ______________________________

Suspenseful ______________________________

Believable characters ______________________________

Would you recommend this book? Yes No Maybe

# My Review and Thoughts

# Book Details

Title: ______________________

Subtitle: ______________________

Author: ______________________

Genre: ______________ #Pages________

Series: ______________________

How many in series? ______________

Next book in series ______________

Format: Print E-Book Audio PDF

Bought/Borrowed from ______________

Date started ____________ Finished __________

How would you rate this book?

Fill in the mini books - 1= Poor and 5 = Excellent

This book made me feel...

Happy Sad Angry Grateful Loving Disturbed

In your opnion rate the following...

Quality of writing ______________

Engaging plot ______________

Suspenseful ______________

Believable characters ______________

Would you recommend this book? Yes No Maybe

# My Review and Thoughts

# Book Details

**Title:** ______________________________

Subtitle: ______________________________

Author: ______________________________

Genre: ____________________ #Pages __________

Series: ______________________________

How many in series? ____________________

Next book in series ____________________

Format: Print E-Book Audio PDF

Bought/Borrowed from ____________________

Date started ____________ Finished ____________

How would you rate this book?

Fill in the mini books - 1= Poor and 5 = Excellent

This book made me feel...

Happy Sad Angry Grateful Loving Disturbed

In your opnion rate the following...

Quality of writing ____________________

Engaging plot ____________________

Suspenseful ____________________

Believable characters ____________________

Would you recommend this book? Yes No Maybe

# My Review and Thoughts

# Book Details

**Title:** ______________________________

Subtitle: ______________________________

Author: ______________________________

Genre: ____________________ #Pages__________

Series: ______________________________

How many in series? ______________________

Next book in series ______________________

Format: Print E-Book Audio PDF

Bought/Borrowed from ____________________

Date started ______________ Finished __________

How would you rate this book?

Fill in the mini books - 1= Poor and 5 = Excellent

This book made me feel...

Happy Sad Angry Grateful Loving Disturbed

In your opnion rate the following...

Quality of writing ______________________

Engaging plot ______________________

Suspenseful ______________________

Believable characters ______________________

Would you recommend this book? Yes No Maybe

# My Review and Thoughts

# Book Details

**Title:** ______________________________

Subtitle: ______________________________

Author: ______________________________

Genre: ____________________ #Pages__________

Series: ______________________________

How many in series? ______________________

Next book in series ______________________

Format: Print E-Book Audio PDF

Bought/Borrowed from ______________________

Date started ______________ Finished __________

How would you rate this book?

Fill in the mini books - 1= Poor and 5 = Excellent

This book made me feel...

Happy Sad Angry Grateful Loving Disturbed

In your opnion rate the following...

Quality of writing ______________________

Engaging plot ______________________

Suspenseful ______________________

Believable characters ______________________

Would you recommend this book? Yes No Maybe

# My Review and Thoughts

# Book Details

**Title:** ______________________________

Subtitle: ______________________________

Author: ______________________________

Genre: ____________________ #Pages__________

Series: ______________________________

How many in series? ______________________

Next book in series ______________________

Format: Print E-Book Audio PDF

Bought/Borrowed from ____________________

Date started ______________ Finished __________

How would you rate this book?

Fill in the mini books - 1= Poor and 5 = Excellent

This book made me feel...

Happy Sad Angry Grateful Loving Disturbed

In your opnion rate the following...

Quality of writing ______________________

Engaging plot ______________________

Suspenseful ______________________

Believable characters ______________________

Would you recommend this book? Yes No Maybe

# My Review and Thoughts

# Book Details

**Title:** ______________________________

Subtitle: ______________________________

Author: ______________________________

Genre: ____________________ #Pages__________

Series: ______________________________

How many in series? ____________________

Next book in series ____________________

Format: Print E-Book Audio PDF

Bought/Borrowed from ____________________

Date started ______________ Finished __________

How would you rate this book?

Fill in the mini books - 1= Poor and 5 = Excellent

This book made me feel...

Happy Sad Angry Grateful Loving Disturbed

In your opnion rate the following...

Quality of writing ____________________

Engaging plot ____________________

Suspenseful ____________________

Believable characters ____________________

Would you recommend this book? Yes No Maybe

# My Wish List

Title: ______________________________

Author: ______________________________

Series: ______________________________

Store: ______________________________

Library: ______________________________

Date aquired: ______________________________

Title: ______________________________

Author: ______________________________

Series: ______________________________

Store: ______________________________

Library: ______________________________

Date aquired: ______________________________

Title: ______________________________

Author: ______________________________

Series: ______________________________

Store: ______________________________

Library: ______________________________

Date aquired: ______________________________

Title: ______________________________

Author: ______________________________

Series: ______________________________

Store: ______________________________

Library: ______________________________

Date aquired: ______________________________

# More Wishes

Title: ____________________

Author: ____________________

Series: ____________________

Store: ____________________

Library: ____________________

Date aquired: ____________________

Title: ____________________

Author: ____________________

Series: ____________________

Store: ____________________

Library: ____________________

Date aquired: ____________________

Title: ____________________

Author: ____________________

Series: ____________________

Store: ____________________

Library: ____________________

Date aquired: ____________________

Title: ____________________

Author: ____________________

Series: ____________________

Store: ____________________

Library: ____________________

Date aquired: ____________________

# My Personal Notes

# More Notes

# About the Author

Susan A. Jennings was born in Britain of a Canadian mother and British father. Both her Canadian and British heritages are often featured in her stories. She lives in Ottawa, Canada where she writes, historical fiction, women's fiction and contemporary later in life romance. She has published numerous short stories and contributed to several anthologies and dabbled a little with nonfiction. Susan's most recent nonfiction is a book with photographs complied of blogs written by her dog Miss Penny. Susan is also past president of the Ottawa Independent Writers (OIW)

# More Books By Susan

## The Sackville Hotel Trilogy

Book 1 - The Blue Pendant
Book 2 - Anna's Legacy
Book 3 - Sarah's Choice
Box Set - All three books
Prequel – Ruins in Silk*

## Sophie's War Series

Book 1 - Prelude to Sophie's War
Book 2 - Heart of Sophie's War
Book 3 - In the Wake of Sophie's War (2022)
Prequel - Ruins in Silk *
*Leads into The Blue Pendant and Sophie's War

## The Lavender Cottage Books

Book 1 - When Love Ends Romance Begins
Book 2 - Christmas at Lavender Cottage
Book 3 - Believing Her Lies
Book 4 - Second Chances

## Nonfiction

Save Some for me - A Memoir
A Book Tracking Journal for ladies
Forget-Me-Not A Book Tracking Journal
A Dog with a Blog - Miss Penny Speaking

## Short Stories:

Mr. Booker's Book Shop
The Tiny Man
A Grave Secret
Gillian's Ghostly Dilemma
The Angel Card
Little Dog Lost Reiki Found

## Story Collections

The Blue Heron Mysteries
Contributing author to:
The Black Lake Chronicles
Ottawa Independent Writers' Anthologies

Made in the USA
Coppell, TX
10 December 2022

88527945R00075